Spy Files

SECRET AGENTS

Adrian Gilbert

QEB Publishing

Copyright © QEB Publishing, Inc. 2008

Published in the United States by
QEB Publishing, Inc.
23062 La Cadena Drive
Laguna Hills, CA 92653

www.qeb-publishing.com

Library of Congress Control Number: 2008010030

ISBN 978 1 59566 592 8

Printed and bound in the United States

Author Adrian Gilbert
Consultant Clive Gifford
Editor Amanda Askew
Designer Lisa Peacock
Picture Researcher Maria Joannou

Publisher Steve Evans
Creative Director Zeta Davies

Picture credits (t=top, b=bottom, l=left, r=right)
Corbis Bettmann 5t, 5b, 6, 7b, 9t, 12b, 16b, 21t, 23tr, 27t, 27b, Columbia Pictures/ZUMA 23tl, Cristiano Chiodi/EPA 17t, Hulton-Deutsch Collection 10b, Pawel Libera 18, Richard A Bloom 26, Rune Hellestad 19b, Wally McNamee 25b, Yassukovich 22t
Getty Images AFP 15t, 20b, AFP/Helene Seligman 24b, AFP/STF 28t, CNN 24t, Express 23b, Hulton Archive 9b, Hulton Archive/Keystone 8, Keystone 29, Mandel Ngan 14b, Oleg Klimov 17b, Science Faction 11b, Topical Press Agency 19t, US Air Force/Time Life Pictures 28b
The International Spy Museum 16t
Library of Congress 13t
Photoshot UPPA 13b, 15b
Rex Features Sipa Press 14t
Shutterstock 2l, 2r
The National Archives 8b
Topham Picturepoint 20t, 21b, 25t, RIA Novosti 12t, UPPA 22b, World History Archive 10–11
Werner Forman Archive 4t, 7t

Words in **bold** can be found in the glossary on page 30.

Contents

When did spying begin?

In the past, kings and other leaders used spies to find out secret information. This is **called** espionage.

Usually this information was about other countries. However, sometimes a leader needed to know about his own people. Ancient Greek general, Alexander the Great, secretly opened the mail of his own soldiers to discover what they really thought of his military plans.

▲ Spies were used by Chinese emperors to find out if their subjects were loyal to them.

Top Secret!

In the Bible, Moses sent 12 spies to secretly scout the land of Canaan. They reported back, saying it was fertile, but well guarded.

THE FIRST SPIES

The Chinese Empire and the ancient Egyptians were among the first to have proper spies. Since then, spies have become an important part of many **governments**—the people who run a country. Today, spies try to discover, uncover, and capture enemy secret agents.

"Elizabeth's Spymaster"

Nationality: English

Worked for: Queen Elizabeth I, setting up an espionage system in England and abroad.

Life: Walsingham's spies provided intelligence of the naval fleet, the Spanish Armada, a year before it sailed against England in 1588.

Fate: Remained a key advisor to the Queen, uncovering other plots against her.

Sir Francis Walsingham (1530–1590)

THE PLOT AGAINST ELIZABETH

In 1568, Mary Queen of Scots was imprisoned by Queen Elizabeth I of England. In 1587, Sir Francis Walsingham of the English Secret Service **intercepted** and **decoded** letters to Mary from Anthony Babington. The letters encouraged Mary to escape and **overthrow** Elizabeth, making Mary queen of England instead. Walsingham used the letters to have Mary sentenced to death for **treason**.

◄ Mary Queen of Scots was beheaded on February 8, 1587.

Spies at War

Espionage is important during wartime because each side needs to know when the enemy is planning to attack.

When Julius Caesar was preparing to invade Gaul (modern-day France) in 58 BC, he sent spies to find out the strength of the enemy forces and where they were positioned. This helped him to defeat the Gauls and to add their lands to the Roman Empire.

▲ Julius Caesar looks down on the chief of the Gauls who has just surrendered to the Romans. Caesar had him executed.

IN THE NEW WORLD

During the American Civil War (1861–1865), spies played a key role for both sides, the Union and Confederates. As they were both American and spoke the same language, spies were difficult to discover and so were often very successful.

Top Secret!

Before his battle against the Danish at Edington, England, in AD 878, the Saxon King Alfred disguised himself as a musician. He wandered through their camp to discover their plans.

MEN IN BLACK

In the 14th century, Japanese spies called Ninjas became widely used for investigating enemy positions, as well as for special missions, including **sabotage** and **assassination**. They were trained to work without being seen. They usually wore all-black clothing and often worked at nighttime.

◄ A Ninja fighter prepares to draw his sword. Ninjas were used for spying missions because they could work without being discovered.

"America's First Spy"

Nationality: American

Worked for: the United States against the British.

Life: Working **undercover** in British-occupied New York, Hale was recognized by a British officer and arrested in September 1776.

Fate: Hanged by the British for spying. Standing on the **gallows** he said, "I regret that I have but one life to lose for my country."

Nathan Hale (1755–1776)

Spying in World War II

During World War II (1939–1945), secret agents were often ordered to find out when and where a major enemy attack might be made.

Soviet spies were very good at discovering German and Japanese military plans. The Germans were fooled by **Allied** spies about the time and place of the vital US and British landings in Normandy, France, in June 1944.

▲ *A French woman who was accused of working for the Germans during the war had her hair cut off as punishment.*

"Brilliant Double Agent"

Nationality: Spanish

Worked for: British **intelligence**, but pretended to work for the Germans.

Career: He sent the Germans false radio messages about the effect of bombing on Britain and the location of the Normandy landings in France.

Fate: The Germans awarded him the Iron Cross, which he added to his MBE from the British! After the war he went to live in Venezuela.

Juan Pujol (1912–1988)

"The Baseball Spy"

Nationality: American

Worked for: American **OSS** against the Germans.

Career: After a successful career as a major-league baseball player, Berg was sent to help the Yugoslav **Resistance**, and then find out more about the German atom-bomb project.

Fate: He briefly worked for the **CIA** before retiring from spying.

Top Secret!

In 1944, Moe Berg attended a lecture and was given orders to shoot top German scientist Werner von Heisenberg if he mentioned that Germany was close to making an atom bomb.

Moe Berg (1902–1972)

FIGHTING BACK

The Allies also helped countries that had been beaten by Germany to fight against their occupiers. The British **SOE** and the American OSS trained and organized Resistance movements in countries such as France and Yugoslavia. They provided them with guns, explosives, and radios. SOE and OSS agents sometimes took part in the fighting.

◄ Armed with weapons provided by the SOE, French Resistance fighters prepare to ambush the Germans.

Spying in the Cold War

In 1945, at the end of World War II, the world was divided into the Communist **East, led by the** Soviet Union, **and the** Capitalist **West, led by the United States.**

The conflict between the two sides came to be called the Cold War because both sides decided not to physically fight (a "hot" war). This was because war had become too deadly, especially when both sides were armed with **nuclear weapons**.

Klaus Fuchs (1911–1988)

"Chief Atom Spy"

Nationality: German-born Briton

Worked for: KGB against Britain and the United States.

Life: He was a physicist working on the Anglo-American atom-bomb project. He passed important information to the Soviet Union.

Fate: Arrested by the British in 1950, he served nine years in prison before moving to East Germany.

ALLIANCES

Spies found out the other side's weaknesses and persuaded governments of other countries to join them in **alliances**. In the Middle East, Israel was supported by the United States, while its Arab enemies were given weapons and equipment by the Soviet Union.

◄ *The terrible devastation caused by the atomic explosion in the Japanese city of Hiroshima on August 6, 1945.*

THE ATOM-BOMB SPIES

After World War II, only the United States had an **atom bomb**. Soviet intelligence was desperate to find information on the atom bomb to help their own scientists build nuclear weapons.

▲ *A copy of the atom bomb that was dropped on Nagasaki, Japan, on August 9, 1945.*

THE SOVIET BOMB

American and British scientists who worked for Soviet intelligence provided information so the Soviet bomb could be made two years earlier than expected. They exploded their first bomb in August 1949. Soviet spies also found out that America did not have enough bombs to start a nuclear war against them until at least 1950.

Female spies

In the past, women were often considered weak and helpless. This gave them a good cover for spying.

During World War II, the British SOE found that female agents were less likely to be stopped and searched than men. They were used as **couriers** to carry secret information.

◄ A German spy dressed as a poor woman was caught by Russian farmers.

WOMEN SPIES TODAY

Since the end of World War II, women have played an important part within most spying organizations. In 1992, Stella Rimington became the first woman to be head of Britain's **MI5**, while CIA agents Jeanne Vertefeuille and Sandy Grimes led the hunt for CIA traitor Aldrich Ames.

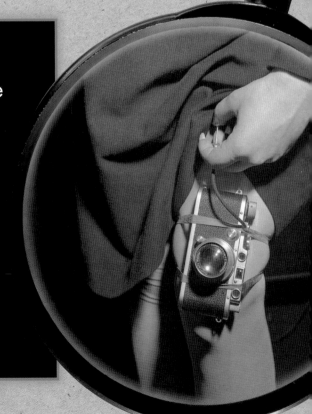

► A camera hidden under the skirt of a female spy. She is about to press the button to take a photograph.

Rose Greenhow (1817–1864)

"Society Spy"

Nationality: American

Worked for: Confederates in the American Civil War.

Career: Well known in Washington D.C., she used her connections with enemy Union generals and politicians to pass on information to the Confederates.

Fate: Caught by the Union, she was briefly imprisoned before being **deported** in 1862.

Top Secret!

Before her execution, Mata Hari ordered a new dress and gloves. She refused a blindfold and blew a kiss to the 12-man firing squad.

"Entertainer"

Nationality: Dutch, but based in France

Worked for: France in World War I (1914–1918).

Career: As she had known many important German officers before 1914, the French asked her to travel to Germany and spy on them.

Fate: The French became suspicious that she was also working for the Germans. She was tried for treason and shot.

Mata Hari (1876–1917)

US secret services

After World War II, the United States split its secret services into three separate organizations.

The Central Intelligence Agency, or CIA, collects secret information from other countries. The Federal Bureau of Investigation, or FBI, is responsible for **counter-intelligence**—catching enemy spies working in the United States. The National Security Agency, or NSA, creates codes for the USA and discovers and breaks enemy codes.

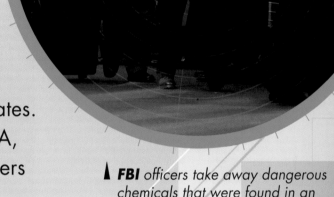

▲ **FBI** officers take away dangerous chemicals that were found in an office in New York in 2007.

POWERFUL ORGANIZATIONS

During the Cold War, the three American secret services became so powerful that they influenced the decisions of the U.S. President. The CIA was also involved in wars against governments in Africa, Asia, and Central America, which they tried to remove from power.

◄ The seal of the Federal Bureau of Investigation. The organization's motto is "Fidelity, Bravery, Integrity."

Allen Dulles (1893–1969)

"CIA Leader"

Nationality: American

Worked for: CIA – director from 1953 to 1961.

Life: Ordered **coups** against the governments of Iran and Guatemala in the 1950s.

Fate: Was responsible for the failed attempt to overthrow Fidel Castro's communist government in Cuba in 1961. He was sacked soon afterwards.

"FBI's Public Face"

Nationality: American

Worked for: FBI—director from 1924 onward.

Life: He built up the FBI and became very important. He was strongly against Communism.

Fate: He was considered too powerful to sack, so he remained at the FBI until his death at the age of 77.

J Edgar Hoover (1895–1972)

Soviet secret services

The first Soviet secret service was called the Cheka, and this organization developed into the all-powerful KGB, the Russian abbreviation for Committee for State Security.

▲ *A single-shot pistol hidden in a lipstick case was an assassination weapon used by the KGB.*

Top Secret!
In the 1980s, the KGB had more than 400,000 people working for it—half of them were border guards who stopped people escaping from the country.

The KGB was responsible for keeping the Soviet Union safe, as well as finding information abroad. The KGB employed many **informers**, making it difficult for foreign spies to work in the Soviet Union.

"Iron Felix"

Nationality: Russian with Polish background

Worked for: Founder of the Cheka.

Life: A brilliant counter-intelligence chief, he quickly put a stop to activities against the new Soviet government.

Fate: He died of a stroke during an argument with the Soviet ruler, Joseph Stalin.

Felix Dzerzhinsky (1877–1926)

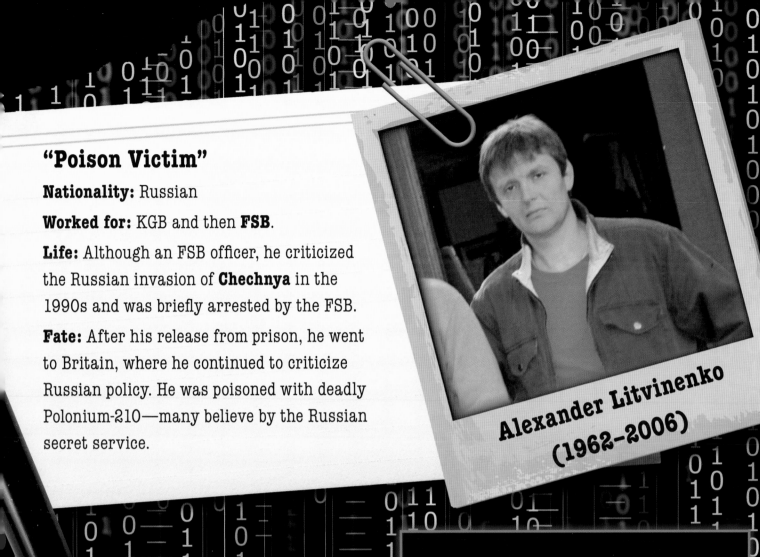

"Poison Victim"

Nationality: Russian

Worked for: KGB and then **FSB**.

Life: Although an FSB officer, he criticized the Russian invasion of **Chechnya** in the 1990s and was briefly arrested by the FSB.

Fate: After his release from prison, he went to Britain, where he continued to criticize Russian policy. He was poisoned with deadly Polonium-210—many believe by the Russian secret service.

Alexander Litvinenko
(1962-2006)

A NEW SERVICE

In 1992, the KGB was shut down and replaced with two organizations. The FSB is responsible for security within Russia, and the **SVR** looks after foreign intelligence. Russian President Vladimir Putin was head of the FSB from July 1998 to August 1999.

◄ In 2006, the FSB discovered a hollowed-out rock outside their offices in Moscow, Russia. It contained a **transmitter**, which many believe was used by Britain's **MI6**.

British secret services

The British secret services are divided into three separate organizations, similar to that of the Americans.

The Security Service, or MI5, is responsible for preventing spying and **terrorism**. The Secret Intelligence Service (SIS), or MI6, collects secret information from around the world. The Government Communications Headquarters (GCHQ) is responsible for collecting and interpreting signals intelligence (**Sigint**) as well as breaking enemy codes and providing codes for British intelligence.

Top Secret!

Mansfield Cumming signed his letters with a "C," and since than all leaders of MI6 have been known as "C."

The London headquarters of MI6 on the River Thames is known as "Legoland."

"Founder of MI6"

Nationality: British

Worked for: First chief of MI6, from 1909 to 1923.

Life: He had a leg amputated after a car accident in 1914, and from then on used a child's scooter to speed around the corridors of his offices in Whitehall.

Fate: He died peacefully while in charge of MI6.

Captain Sir Mansfield Cumming (1859–1923)

Stella Rimington (1935–)

"Female Spy Chief"

Nationality: British

Worked for: MI5, as Director General.

Life: Not only was she the first female head of MI5, but she also gave the public more information about MI5 than ever before.

Fate: In 1996, she retired from MI5 and has since written several spy novels.

Spy rings

Many spies work alone, sending secret information to their handler.

However, it is better for spies to work in small rings, or groups, with each person having a different skill. Often they will not know each other, and all communication goes through the handler.

▲ Heinz Felfe, the leader of a Soviet spy ring, is taken into court. He was charged with stealing secrets from West Germany in 1963.

RED RINGS

Soviet intelligence was good at developing spy rings. It set up the Red Orchestra Ring in Germany during World War II. The Soviet Atom Spy Ring was formed during and after the war. It involved many spies, couriers, and handlers in the United States and Britain.

Top Secret!
One of the Cambridge Spy Ring, art historian Anthony Blunt, was honored by the Queen with a knighthood before being unmasked as a spy in 1979.

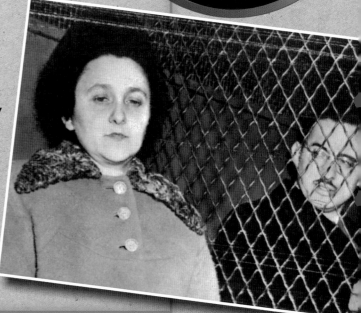

► Ethel and Julius Rosenberg were part of the Soviet Atom Spy Ring in the United States. They were caught by the FBI and sentenced to death for treason in 1953.

"The Ultimate Mole"

Nationality: British

Worked for: Soviet Intelligence against Britain.

Life: He began working for the Soviets in the 1930s and joined MI5 in 1939.

Fate: In 1951, he was forced to leave MI6. In 1963, he fled to the Soviet Union and spent the rest of his life there.

Kim Philby (1912–1988)

THE CAMBRIDGE SPY RING

During the 1930s, Soviet intelligence used many wealthy British people who did not like the way Britain was run. They hid their dislike and worked hard. Eventually, they were given important jobs in Britain where they could find information for the Soviets. They were known as **moles**.

The Cambridge Spy Ring involved five former students of Cambridge University, England, who acted as moles. They were Kim Philby, Anthony Burgess, Donald Maclean, Anthony Blunt, and John Caincross.

◄ Clockwise from the top left: Anthony Blunt, Guy Burgess, Donald Maclean, and Kim Philby. They all gained access to important British secrets that were passed to Soviet intelligence.

Spy writers

Spy fiction has always been popular. Spy novels feature adventure, dark deeds, and a hero fighting a ruthless enemy.

Most writers of spy fiction just use their imagination to write their stories. However, a few have been spies themselves.

◄ *One of the Aston Martin sports cars used by James Bond. One model had an ejector seat to get rid of unwanted passengers!*

COLD WAR CAPERS

British novelist Graham Greene worked for MI6 during World War II, and he used some of his experiences as a spy in his novels set in the Cold War. Charles McCarry used knowledge from when he worked for the CIA in his Paul Christopher series of spy novels.

◄ *Some of the most realistic Cold War novels have been written by John le Carré, who worked for both MI5 and MI6.*

"The Ultimate Movie Spy"
James Bond (1952–)

Nationality: British

Worked for: MI6

Life: With a **licence to kill**, there have been six actors in the official Bond films, including Sean Connery and Daniel Craig.

Fate: Bond continues to fight against the enemy. His enemies may change but Bond is the best.

CAMERA 160 60997   CAMERA 160 60997

001   002

THE NAME'S BOND

The most famous spy of all is, of course, James Bond, 007. His creator, Ian Fleming, was employed by British naval intelligence during World War II. Several characters in the 13 novels he wrote are based on people he worked with, although Bond himself was a fictional creation.

◄ Ian Fleming was the author of the highly successful series of James Bond spy novels.

Spy catching

One of the main duties of a secret service is to catch enemy spies and stop them from working. Organizations such as the FBI in the United States and MI5 in Britain are responsible for counter-intelligence.

In the Soviet Union, Smersh—an abbreviation of the Russian "Death to Spies"—was set up to stop **opposition** during and after World War II.

▲ US counter-intelligence expert Robert Hanssen is arrested by the FBI after spying for Russia.

TERRORIST THREATS

More recently, terrorism has become a dangerous threat. The British secret services fought for a long time against the IRA, the Irish Republican Army. In the 21st century, **militant** Islamic organizations, such as al-Qaeda, have become the chief target of Western counter-intelligence organizations.

◀ The Twin Towers of the World Trade Center in New York were hit by two aircraft on September 11, 2001. The planes were piloted by militant Islamic terrorists.

THE MAN IN THE TRUNK

Mordecai Louk was a **double agent** working for both Egypt and Israel. The Egyptians were suspicious of Louk, however, and decided to catch him in Cairo. They gave him drugs to make him sleepy and hid him in a trunk ready to fly back to Egypt.

After a delay at an Italian airport, the drugs wore off and Italian customs officers heard muffled cries from the trunk. The Egyptian agents tried to escape with the trunk, but it was opened and Louk was released. Louk was then sent back to Israel, where he was put in prison for ten years for spying for Egypt!

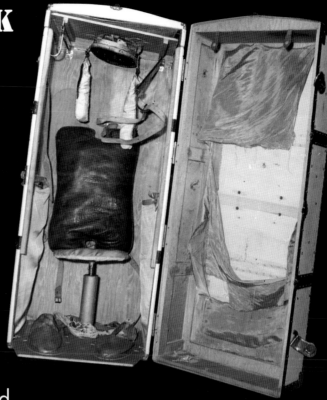

The trunk used by Egyptian intelligence to carry Mordecai Louk back to Egypt.

"The Spy Hunter"

Nationality: American

Life: One of the founders of the CIA, Angleton was also regarded as a brilliant spy catcher.

Fate: After **debriefing** Soviet **defector**, Anatoliy Golitsyn, Angleton thought that the CIA had been **infiltrated** by the KGB. He began a hunt to find these possible Soviet spies. This annoyed many people in the CIA and, in 1974, he was forced to resign.

James Angleton (1917–1987)

Spying for money

Some people, such as Kim Philby or Klaus Fuchs, spied against their country because they believed it was the right thing to do. Others simply wanted money.

▲ Aldrich Ames leaves court after admitting spying for the KGB. He was sentenced to life imprisonment.

John Walker and Aldrich Ames sold secrets to the Soviet Union to pay for their expensive lifestyles. Ames worked for CIA counter-intelligence and was thought to be particularly damaging to the United States. Before he was caught in 1994, he told the KGB about Russian intelligence officers who were actually spying for the United States. At least ten of them were then executed.

TOP SPY

Walker was a communications specialist in the U.S. Navy who, from 1968 to 1985, provided Soviet intelligence with thousands of **classified** naval messages. He was one of the most successful Soviet spies in recent U.S. history.

Top Secret!

John Walker attempted to recruit his daughter Laura into his spy ring when she was serving in the US Army, but she refused.

A FAMILY BUSINESS

Unusually for a spy, Walker did not work alone. He developed his own spy ring with his brother Arthur, son Michael, and friend Jerry Whitworth. They all had connections with the U.S. Navy, too. However, his ex-wife Barbara reported him to the FBI. He was arrested in 1985 after he was caught leaving 129 documents at a **dead drop** in Maryland for the KGB.

▲ Michael Walker was given a 25-year prison sentence in 1985, but he was released in 2000.

John Walker (1937–)

"The Submarine Spy"

Nationality: American

Worked for: KGB against the U.S. Navy.

Life: Provided Soviet intelligence with knowledge of the U.S. nuclear submarine fleet and of its undersea movements.

Fate: Arrested by the FBI in 1985, he was sentenced to life imprisonment.

Spy swaps

When spies are caught, they can expect harsh treatment, which can mean torture and death.

The Soviet Union executed enemy spies who were Soviet citizens. Foreign enemy spies were usually imprisoned so they could be used in exchange for Soviet spies caught in other countries.

Soviet **dissident**, Anatoli Sharansky (in hat), is released on Berlin's Glienicke bridge in Germany – the place of many spy exchanges.

FAMOUS SPY SWAP

The first famous spy swap involved CIA pilot Francis Gary Powers and KGB agent Colonel Rudolf Abel. Powers was shot down whilst flying a U-2 spy plane over the Soviet Union in 1961. Abel was a top agent who had run a spy ring in the United States. Each side wanted their man back, and in February 1962, an exchange was made in Berlin, Germany.

◄ Francis Gary Powers prepares to board his aircraft before the mission over the Soviet Union.

KGB AND MI6 EXCHANGE

Another top KGB officer Konon Molody was exchanged in 1964 for Greville Wynne, a British businessman who worked for MI6 in the Soviet Union. In 1962, Wynne was caught collecting material from Soviet military officer Oleg Penkovsky. At their trial, Wynne received a prison sentence, but Penkovsky was sentenced to death.

◄ Greville Wynne arrives in Britain in April 1964, after his spy swap with Konon Molody in Berlin, Germany.

Top Secret!

Between 1964 and 1989, West Germany paid East Germany around $2.4 billion to make sure 33,755 political prisoners and 215,019 other East Germans were released.

PROTECTION

Many spies have **diplomatic status**, so they cannot be punished for breaking the law in another country. If a spy is caught, they will normally be questioned for a short while and then sent back to their home country.

GLOSSARY

Alliance A group of countries working with each other against another country or group of countries.

Allies/Allied The World War II alliance between Britain, the Soviet Union, and the USA (and other, smaller countries) against Germany, Japan, and Italy.

Assassination The targeted killing of an individual, especially by a secret organization.

Atom bomb A very powerful bomb in which uranium or plutonium atoms are split, producing an enormous release of energy.

Capitalist A person or economic system that is based on the power and ownership of money and property.

Chechnya A state in the southern part of the former Soviet Union that broke away from Russia, leading to war between Russia and Chechnya during the 1990s.

CIA Central Intelligence Agency, the intelligence-collecting organization of the USA.

Classified Secret, especially a document.

Communist A person or system based on the idea that the government owns and controls all property.

Counter-intelligence The tracking down of enemy spies in one's own country.

Coup The violent overthrow of a government by a small group against that government.

Courier A member of a spy ring who carries secret information from place to place, usually without knowing what it is.

Dead drop A place where a spy leaves secret material to be picked up by a controller or another spy.

Debriefing A series of interviews where a spy tells the controller all they know.

Decoding Finding out what is contained in a secret message.

Defector A person who has decided to work for an opposing country or intelligence organization.

Deport To be made to leave a country.

Diplomatic status Spies working directly from their embassy abroad are given special privileges that mean they cannot be imprisoned or executed if they are caught spying.

Dissident A person who disagrees with their government. In many countries, they are punished and sent to prison.

Double agent A spy working for two intelligence organizations at the same time. The spy is loyal to one side and pretending to be loyal to the other.

Espionage Spying to find out information.

Execution When someone is killed as punishment.

FBI Federal Bureau of Investigation, the security service of the USA.

FSB The security service of the Russian Federation.

Gallows A structure—often made from wood—from which a noose is suspended, and used for execution by hanging.

Government A group of people who rule a country or state.

Handler Another word for a controller—an agent who directs and supports spies working undercover.

Infiltrate To secretly enter another country or organization.

Informer A person who secretly provides information against another person.

Intelligence Organization that seeks secret information.

Intercept To get hold of information that is not intended for you.

KGB The combined security and intelligence services of the Soviet Union.

Licence to kill An expression made popular in the James Bond spy novels and films, giving a spy the legal right to kill another spy.

MI5 Military Intelligence Section 5, the security service of Great Britain.

MI6 Military Intelligence Section 6, the intelligence service of Great Britain.

Militant A person with an aggressive belief in their cause.

Mole A spy who spends a long time working their way into an enemy organization before beginning any spying activities.

Nuclear weapon A general term for atom or hydrogen bombs and missiles.

Opposition Strong disagreement with a plan, law, or system.

OSS Office of Strategic Studies, an intelligence and special operations organization formed by the USA during World War II.

Overthrow To remove a leader from power.

Resistance A secret organization that attacks an occupying army using tactics such as sabotage.

Sabotage The secret destruction of enemy equipment, often by civilians.

Sigint An abbreviation for signals intelligence—information gained by listening in to enemy electronic transmissions, such as radio, telephones, or e-mail.

SOE Special Operations Executive, an undercover special operations and sabotage organization set up by Britain to attack the Germans in Occupied Europe.

Soviet Union A country in Europe and Asia, between 1917 and 1991.

SVR The foreign intelligence service of the Russian Federation.

Terrorism The use of violence, usually against civilians, to create fear and to make a government do something.

Transmitter Equipment that sends out radio or television signals.

Treason The act of secretly working to overthrow or betray your own country.

Undercover Working in enemy territory while pretending to be someone else.

INDEX